WEEKLY WR READER®

EARLY LEARNING LIBRARY

Seasons of the Year

Autumn

by JoAnn Early Macken

Reading consultant: Susan Nations, M.Ed.,
author, literacy coach,
and consultant in literacy development

Please visit our web site at: www.earlyliteracy.cc
For a free color catalog describing Weekly Reader® Early Learning Library's list
of high-quality books, call 1-877-445-5824 (USA) or 1-800-387-3178 (Canada).
Weekly Reader® Early Learning Library's fax: (414) 336-0164.

Library of Congress Cataloging-in-Publication Data

Macken, JoAnn Early, 1953-
    Autumn / by JoAnn Early Macken.
      p. cm. – (Seasons of the year)
      ISBN 0-8368-6353-4 (lib. bdg.)
      ISBN 0-8368-6358-5 (softcover)
      1. Autumn—Juvenile literature. I. Title.
    QB637.7.M33   2006
    508.2–dc22   2005025075

This edition first published in 2006 by
Weekly Reader® Early Learning Library
A Member of the WRC Media Family of Companies
330 West Olive Street, Suite 100
Milwaukee, WI 53212 USA

Editor: Dorothy L. Gibbs
Art direction: Tammy West
Cover design and page layout: Kami Strunsee
Picture research: Cisley Celmer

Photo credits: Cover, © Myrleen Ferguson Cate/PhotoEdit; p. 4 © Mary
Steinbacher/PhotoEdit; p. 5 © Michael Newman/PhotoEdit; p. 6 © age
fotostock/SuperStock; p. 7 © Mitch York/Getty Images; p. 8 © Nancy Sheehan/
PhotoEdit; pp. 9, 14, 15 Gregg Andersen; p. 10 © Robert W. Ginn/PhotoEdit;
pp. 11, 12 © Gibson Stock Photography; p. 13 © George Haling/Photo
Researchers, Inc; p. 16 (all) © Hemera

Printed in the United States of America

1 2 3 4 5 6 7 8 9 10 09 08 07 06

Note to Educators and Parents

Learning to read is one of the most exciting and challenging things young children do. Among other skills, they are beginning to match the spoken word to print and learn directionality and print conventions. Books that are appropriate for emergent readers will incorporate many of these conventions while also being appealing and entertaining.

The books in the *Seasons of the Year* series are designed to support young readers in the earliest stages of literacy. They will love looking at the full color photographs while learning about the exciting world of seasonal changes and differences. Each book will invite children to read—and reread—again and again!

In addition to serving as wonderful picture books in schools, libraries, and homes, this series is specifically intended to be read within instructional small groups. The small group setting enables the teacher or other adult to provide scaffolding that will boost the reader's efforts. Children and adults alike will find these books supportive, engaging, and fun!

–Susan Nations, M.Ed., author, literacy coach,
and consultant in literacy development

Autumn is cool.

The wind blows.

Leaves change.

Leaves fall.

We rake.

We jump.

We run.

We kick.

We pick apples.

We pick
pumpkins.

We eat pie.

Yum!

Glossary

apples

pie

leaves

pumpkins